WHAT IS
Hope?

SOME OTHER BOOKS BY VARDELL & WONG

What Is a FRIEND?

What Is a FAMILY?

Things We Do

Things We Eat

Things We Feel

GREAT MORNING:
Poems for School Leaders to Read Aloud

HERE WE GO:
A Poetry Friday Power Book

HOP TO IT:
Poems to Get You Moving

The Poetry Friday Anthology
for Celebrations

The Poetry of Science

YOU JUST WAIT:
A Poetry Friday Power Book

WHAT IS Hope?

by
Sylvia Vardell
+
Janet Wong

Pomelo Books

100% of the profits from this book will be donated to the IBBY Children in Crisis Fund.

The IBBY Children in Crisis Fund provides support for children whose lives have been disrupted through war, civil disorder, or natural disaster. The program gives immediate support and help – and also aims for long-term community impact, aligning with IBBY's goal of giving every child the right to become a reader.

ibby.org/awards-activities/ibby-children-in-crisis-fund
usbby.org/donate.html

This book is dedicated to supporters of IBBY all over the world.

Special thanks to Renée M. LaTulippe for her ongoing help in editing Pomelo Books publications.

No part of this publication may be reproduced, or stored in a retrieval system, or transmitted in any form or by any means, electronic, mechanical, photocopying, recording, or otherwise, without written permission of the publisher. For information regarding permission, please contact us:

Pomelo Books
9440 Viewside Drive
Dallas, TX 75231
PomeloBooks.com
info@pomelobooks.com

Text/compilation copyright © 2023 by Pomelo Books. All rights reserved.
Individual poems copyright © 2023 by the individual poets. All rights reserved.
Photos sourced from Canva.com.
Library of Congress Cataloging-in-Publication Data is available.

ISBN 978-1-937057-24-4

Please visit us at PomeloBooks.com

POEMS BY

Verrena Diane Anderson
Dolores Andral
Marcie Flinchum Atkins
Rebecca Balcárcel
Robyn Hood Black
Sandy Brehl
Joseph Bruchac
Rose Cappelli
Kelly Conroy
Patricia Cooley
Cynthia Cotten
Mary E. Cronin
Linda A. Dryfhout
Alyssa Eisner
Joanne Emery
Lauren Emick
Janet Clare Fagal
Patricia J. Franz
Theresa Gaughan
Stephanie Gimble

Sherilyn Howard
Elizabeth Kuelbs
Jone Rush MacCulloch
Vikram Madan
J. David Martinez
Rochelle Melander
Kenn Nesbitt
Abby Oqueli
Lou Piccolo
Deborah Reidy
Suma Subramaniam
Linda Picaro Tarantino
Pamela Taylor
Linda Kulp Trout
Joyce Uglow
Sylvia Vardell
Vicki Wilke
Matthew Winter
Janet Wong
Sarah Ziman

TABLE OF CONTENTS

WORLD by Sylvia Vardell	9
HURRICANE by Sherilyn Howard	11
VOLUNTEER by Sarah Ziman	13
MORNING by Vikram Madan	15
METAMORPHOSIS by Robyn Hood Black	17
FLIGHT by Suma Subramaniam	19
MIGRATION by Vicki Wilke	21
LIGHT by Joseph Bruchac	23
MICROSCOPE by Elizabeth Kuelbs	25
TELESCOPE by Patricia Cooley	27
MAIL by Linda Kulp Trout	29
FORTUNE by Deborah Reidy	31
MONEY by Marcie Flinchum Atkins	33
FISHING by Rose Cappelli	35
SNAP! by Joyce Uglow	37
TUG-OF-WAR by Lauren Emick	39
BENCHMARK by Sandy Brehl	41
DRUM by Mary E. Cronin	43
PROTEST by Stephanie Gimble	45
LIGHTHOUSE by Alyssa Eisner	47
AIRPORT by Linda A. Dryfhout	49
ROCKET by Kelly Conroy	51
SUSPENSE by Kenn Nesbitt	53
PICKLEBALL by Janet Wong	55
ESPERANZA by Joanne Emery	57
BOOKS by Matthew Winter	59
WHEELS by Linda Picaro Tarantino	61
AMBULANCE by Theresa Gaughan	63

TABLE OF CONTENTS

VISITING by Jone Rush MacCulloch	65
SCULPTED by Dolores Ancral	67
HELP! by Cynthia Cotten	69
PLEA by Pamela Taylor	71
ODE by Rochelle Melander	73
MILITARY by Verrena Diane Anderson	75
HIKE by Rebecca Balcárcel	77
SEEDLINGS by Abby Oqueli	79
RAINMAKING by Lou Piccolo	81
TEST by Janet Clare Fagal	83
THANK-U by J. David Martinez	85
WONDER by Patricia J. Franz	87
Resources for Readers + Writers	89
Poetry Books About Hope	90
Ekphrastic Poetry Books	91
Web Resources	92
Sharing Poetry Out Loud	93
Poets Write about Writing	94
Places to Publish Poetry	95
Published Poetry by Young Writers	96
Kinds of Poems	97
Poetry Awards and Best Lists	98
About the Poets	99
Poem Credits	104
About Vardell & Wong	105
About Pomelo Books	106
More from Pomelo Books	107

WORLD
by Sylvia Vardell

I worry
about our world –
all those angry hurricanes,
tornadoes of hate,
and storms of sadness.
But then,
my best friend
makes me laugh out loud,
my dog
wags his poofy tail,
my dad
bakes my favorite cookies
for no reason at all.
Worry won't win –
I hope.

HURRICANE
by Sherilyn Howard

My stomach
Is a hurricane,
Swirling
Twirling
Forceful, gray
Every single
First fall day
Of school.

Seas and Cs
Create such forces
Knocking all
Off chartered courses.
Yet best friends
From class last year
Disrupt the winds
Downgrade my fear.
Make me hopeful
For Day Two.

The storm will pass by
Soon.

VOLUNTEER
by Sarah Ziman

If everybody
did their bit –
stood up,
went out,
   just
started it –
between us all
we'd get things done:
a cleaner world,
a fairer one.
One piece of garbage,
then one more,
one extra minute
than before,
one volunteer
who brings one friend –
a chain of
   hope
that will not end.

MORNING
by Vikram Madan

Brand new
morning,
brand new
start.
Hope
sunrising
in my heart.

METAMORPHOSIS
by Robyn Hood Black

To look at me,
you might only see
my long body bunching up.
Munching leaves.
Lumbering along a branch,
earth bound.

What you don't see
are my wings.

Yet.

They're there.
Give me a little time.
A place to spin.
A thread of hope.

Soon,
I will stretch iridescent wings
and dance in the wandering wind.

FLIGHT
by Suma Subramaniam

Flutter,
glide in circles,
lodge into the sky,
flap your wings across the clouds,
spin, swerve,
wheel, whirl,
swirl, twirl,
soar.
Show the world
how to break free
and fly.

MIGRATION
by Vicki Wilke

We gather
We depart
Stick together
From the start.

Use our strength
Flap new feathers
Work to keep
Our flock together.

Staying close
In V array
We share tailwinds . . .
All the way.

We survive
Our aviation –
With lots of
Honking conversation!

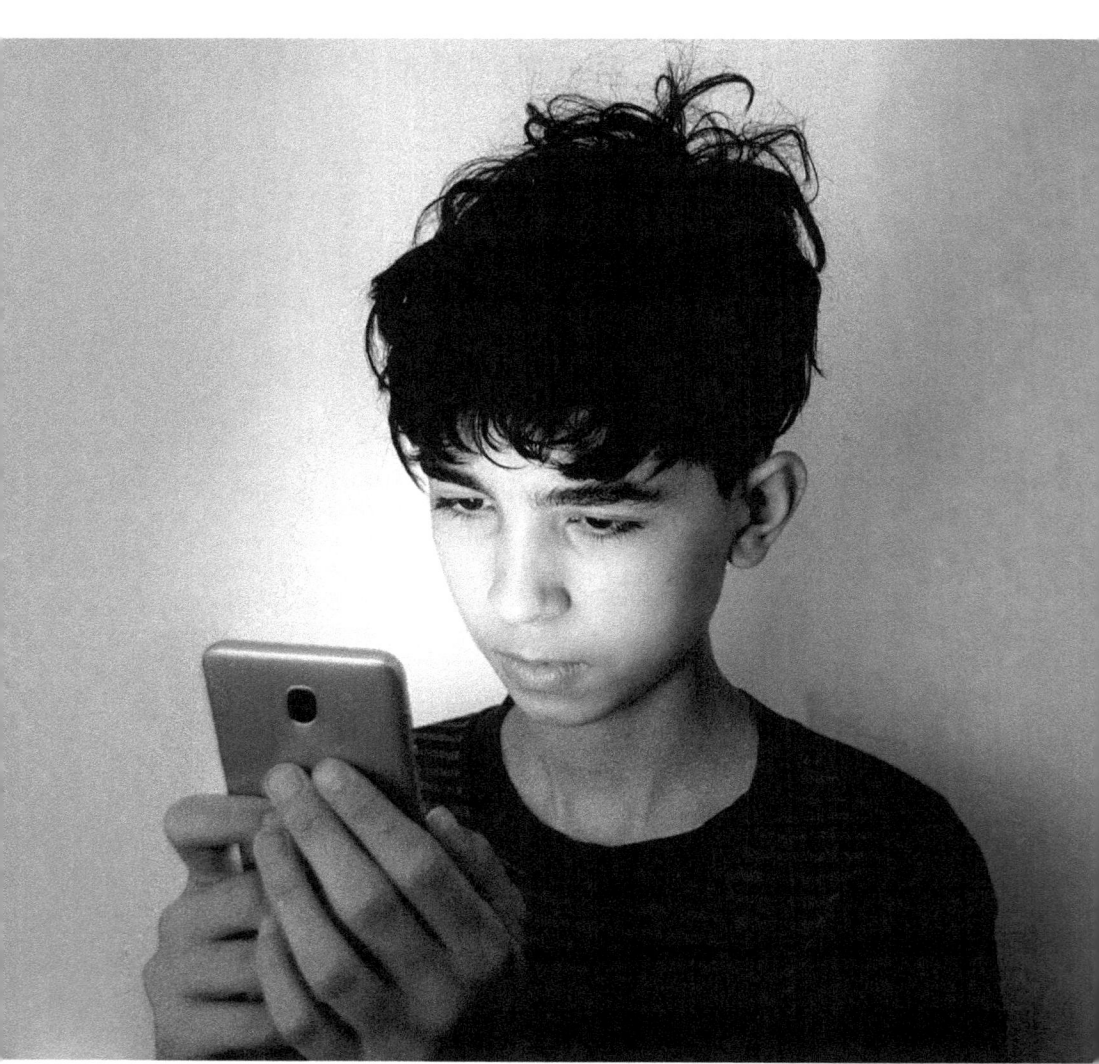

LIGHT
by Joseph Bruchac

What do I see
in the light of my phone?
Not confusion,
but opportunity.

A game I might play,
a new friend I might meet,
a message
from someone
who cares about me.

Or maybe someplace
I might go someday –
a whole world
of possibilities.

And brighter than
anything
shining
from that small screen
is the light
in my
own eyes.

MICROSCOPE
by Elizabeth Kuelbs

I am a light bender. I magnify
microworlds, bounce
photons

through glass
and metal to illuminate
the too-small-to-see. Come –

look through my lenses, sharpen
your focus. I will
show you

a glistening
trove of sugar crystals,
moss piglets paddling in a drip

of pond water, the bright green
cells in your celery stick,
a soap foam

bubble ballet.
What view, I wonder, will
you discover, that no one's ever seen?

TELESCOPE
by Patricia Cooley

When I look
through my telescope,
I see
planets up above,
and it makes
me wonder
if an alien
is looking
through a telescope
down at me.

MAIL
by Linda Kulp Trout

We text each other
almost every day,
but for friends like us
words on a screen
don't seem special enough.

So today
inside your mailbox
you'll find something new,
a handwritten letter
from me to you.

And if you agree
this way is better,
maybe tomorrow
you'll write me
a letter.

FORTUNE
by Deborah Reidy

A little slip of paper
tells all you need to know,
hopes,
dreams,
good luck,
exciting places you might go.

It's right there in your hand
in a crispy cookie fold –
crack,
crunch,
pull it out.
What does the future hold?

MONEY
by Marcie Flinchum Atkins

How much money
did we make?

We want to buy
a slithery snake.

Mom hopes
we don't have enough –

unless the snake we buy
is

STUFFED!

FISHING
by Rose Cappelli

I wait for a tug,
a nibble,
a sign
that something is there
on the end of my line.

It could be a minnow,
a catfish,
a trout.
It could be a walleye
swimming about.

What if it's a treasure
instead of a fish?
A skateboard,
a mermaid,
a ship –

or a wish.

SNAP!
by Joyce Uglow

One unlucky turkey.
Two lucky pullers.
Three minutes to decide.

Ready, set . . .

NOT YET!
Let me think.

I'll wish for no
homework, no
onions, no
peas, and no
early bedtimes.

Shhhh! Wishes
can't be known!
Anyway
I have dreams
of my own.

Ready, set, now!
SNAP!

It's a
perfect clean break!

*A clean break happens when the wishbone breaks evenly. It is said that both wishes will come true.

TUG-OF-WAR
by Lauren Emick

Challengers ready
Step up to the rope
We pull together
To win, we hope.

Two steps forward
One step back
Use your muscles
Stay on track.

Dig your heels in
Make a stand
We won't go down
Pull with both hands.

It's tug-of-war
Between two teams
Pushing, pulling
Grass-stained jeans.

We lurch forward
Is this defeat?
With one last effort
We can't be beat.

BENCHMARK
by Sandy Brehl

TAP. TAP. TAP.

Hands in laps.
Chatter stills.

Sorting files.
Surveying statements.

Scanning scrubbed faces,
Slicked hair, ribbons.
Braids in place.

Promises, privileges,
Problems, pitfalls.
Possibilities.

Adoption: Final.

TAP. TAP. TAP.

DRUM
by Mary E. Cronin

Feel it in our circle –
the cadence,
the thrum.
Feel it in your fingertips,
your palm,
your thumb.

Together we are beat
and echo
and thud.
Feel it in your breath,
feel it in your blood.

Together we are rise
and rhythm
and hum.
Feel it in your chest –
hope is a drum.

PROTEST
by Stephanie Gimble

Sing your protest song
Sing it loud
Sing it strong
Sing until we right what's wrong

Raise your signs up high
Write the words
That must be heard
And raise them to the sky

March one million strong
March in line
Raise your sign
Sing your protest song

LIGHTHOUSE
by Alyssa Eisner

Far from shore
She reaches out.
Trusty signal
Day in, day out.

She keeps the ships from
Running aground.
Daytime, nighttime
All year round.

Nowadays ships
Use GPS.
The lighthouse blinks
Less and less.

Her beacon, though,
Is strong as ever,
Calling tourists
Every summer.

AIRPORT
by Linda A. Dryfhout

There's our airplane. Big white jet.
It's not time to board just yet.

Baggage tram is rolling in.
Bags go in a side door bin.

Time to board. Our pass is scanned.
"How much longer till we land?"

We're buckled in, the engines whine.
Mom says, "You are doing fine."

Time for takeoff. Hold on tight.
My ears pop. It's my first flight.

I can't believe we're up so high.
I settle in. I love to fly!

ROCKET
by Kelly Conroy

When facing brand-new obstacles
has got you stuck or scared,
try this little exercise
to help you feel prepared:

Pretend that you're a rocket ship.
Hear your engines roar.
Count down 5, 4, 3, 2, 1,
then lift off.
        Blast off.
                Soar!

SUSPENSE
by Kenn Nesbitt

I make a wish.
I close my eyes.
I toss my ball.
Away it flies.
I don't know what
my ball will do.
I pray it travels
straight and true.
But, though I hope
with all my might,
I know it could
roll left or right.
It might become
a gutter ball,
or strike the pins
and dash them all.
I hold my breath.
I feel a thrill
like time is stopped
and standing still,
and anything
is possible
the instant that
you toss a ball.

PICKLEBALL
by Janet Wong

Hope rides
on a serve

Hope floats
on a dink

Hope drops
into the kitchen

Hope lands
on the line

Hope puts
its own spin on things

Hope keeps you
in the game

ESPERANZA
by Joanne Emery

Esperanza.
I say the word
three times very slowly:
Esperanza,
Esperanza,
Esperanza –
Four syllables each,
repeated three times,
hope in Spanish.
Again I whisper:
Esperanza,
Esperanza,
Esperanza –
The words form gently
in my mouth
and are released
into the air.
They float bravely away.
I remain here
watching and waiting
for all my wild wishes
I hope will come true.

BOOKS
by Matthew Winter

I love your woodsy
vanilla smell

I love turning your
crisp pages

I love getting lost in
your story

You teach me
so many things

You inspire me and
distract me

You give me strength
and fill me with hope

You show me that
I am not alone.

WHEELS
by Linda Picaro Tarantino

Go, go, go!
I never like
S - L - O - W

Go, go, go!
A slope ahead,
I hope this ride will
L - A - S - T

Go, go, go!
My bike goes very
F A S T –

Go, go, go!
Oh, no . . .
I'm going to
C R A S H !

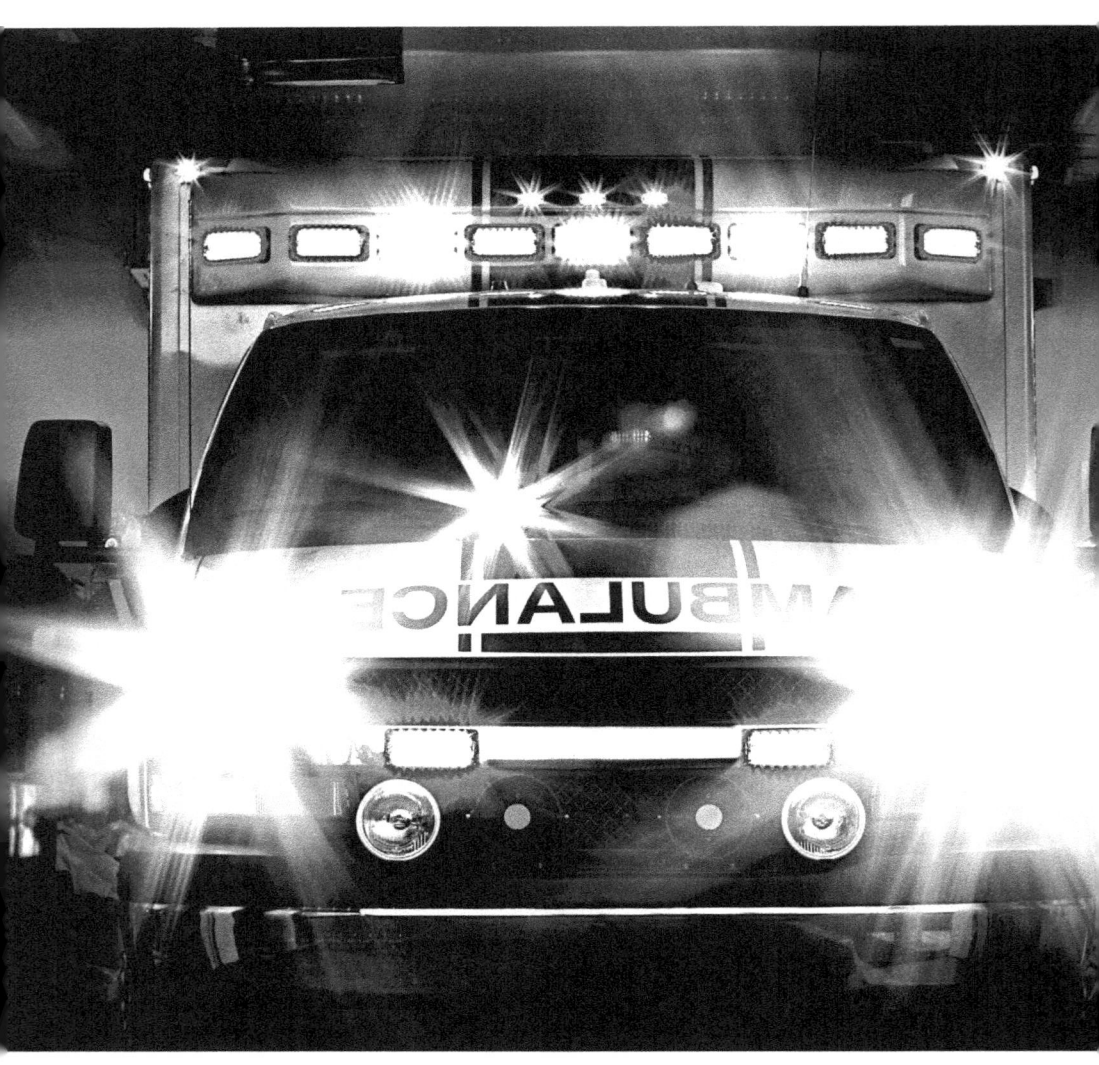

AMBULANCE
by Theresa Gaughan

Rainy night
Scary crash
Help is on the way

Lights flash red
On wet blacktop
Help is on the way

Siren blares
Cars pull aside
Help is on the way

I hope and pray
Everyone's okay
Help is on the way

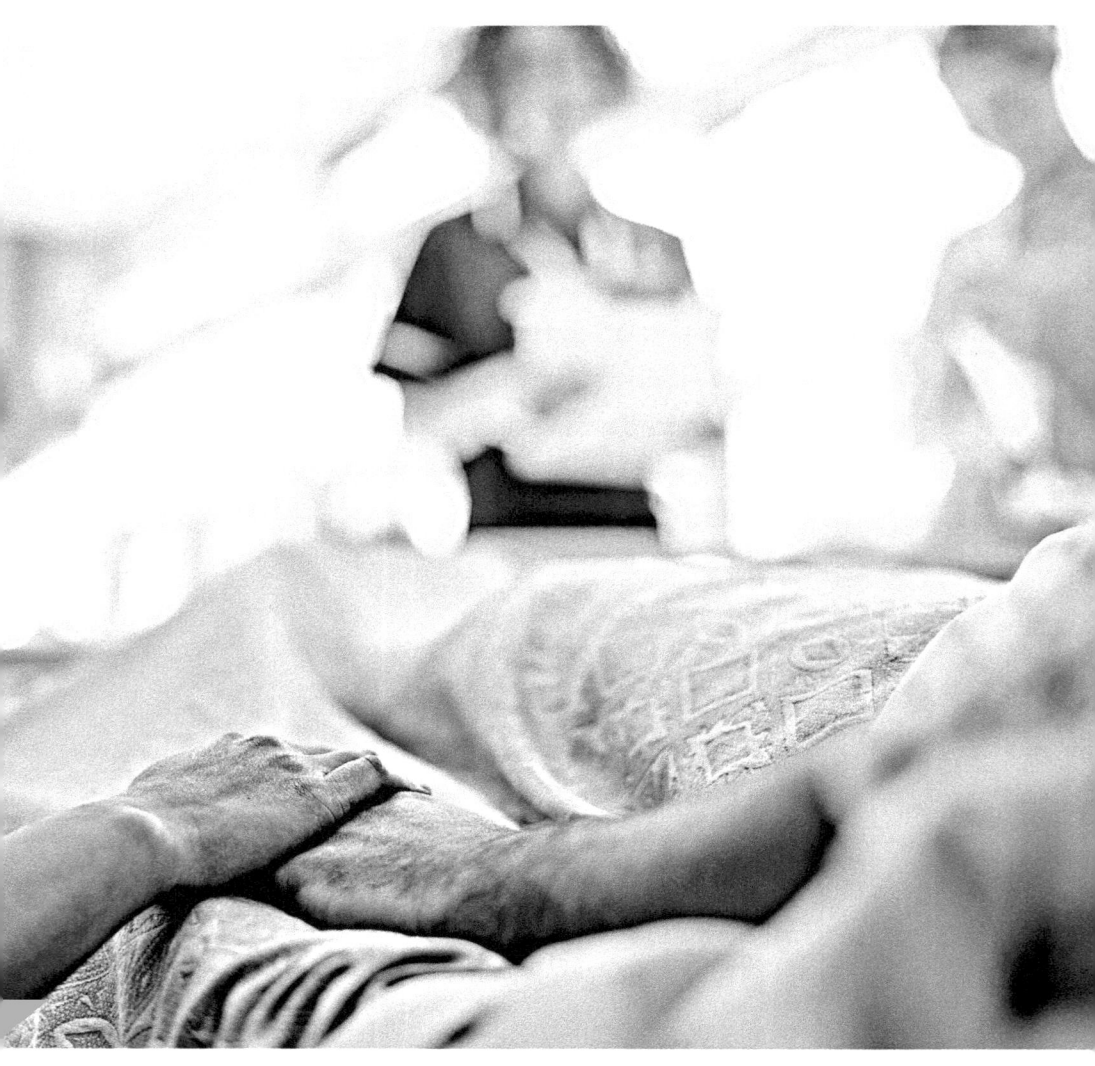

VISITING
by Jone Rush MacCulloch

I hold Grandpa's hand,
grip it gentle, not too hard
I squeeze in Morse code

I-love-you . . . he taught me how
to chatter without speaking

SCULPTED
by Dolores Andral

Hope is carved out of faith
and the essence of hope
can carve out the thoughts
we engrave on our hearts

Hope matters
and with a little matter called hope
we can whittle away our fears
cut the negativity
slash across the misery

Hope, like chalk dust blown
where the sky's the limit,
can't be limited

And as we chisel and score
and shape our outlook
we are encouraged
by the residue

HELP!
by Cynthia Cotten

chased a squirrel
went too far
where am I?

look at me
look *for* me
help me, please

get me home
safe and sound
find me soon

PLEA
by Pamela Taylor

My cat
hopes he will
be okay. The vet
will care for him today.
She'll take his pulse and
check his heart. She'll make
some notes on my cat's chart.
She'll give him meds and
check for fleas. Doctor,
make him better.
Please?

ODE
by Rochelle Melander

Oh, sweet swimmer,
rescued from the sea,
your tailfin flicks –
you remember me.
Your shiny scales,
they glisten.
I whisper my secrets,
you listen.
You stare, I share,
we make a memory.

Note: Goldfish live in freshwater, but some people release their unwanted fish into the wild. This is bad for the fish and the ecosystem. And contrary to popular belief, goldfish have good memories.

MILITARY
by Verrena Diane Anderson

We are an Army family
Soldier
Army mom
Us Army brats and our Army dog

We visit the fort on family day
When the battalion goes to the field
We go in dad's tent
And eat an MRE like soldiers

Military vehicles are on display
Humvees and helicopters
I put on a helmet and climb in
I am a helicopter pilot

On parade day we stand at attention
Salute the flag
Watch the troops march in review
I am proud

We go to my dad's promotion
Now he is a captain
Maybe someday I will be, too –
In the Marines!

HIKE
by Rebecca Balcárcel

Where will you lead me,
where will you lead me,
trail through the leaves?
To giant stones, a squirrel race,
to huffing breath and steady pace.

Where do you lead me,
where do you lead me,
path between the trees?
To frog-song ponds, the fairy's dew,
to tired feet, to summit view.

Where have you led me,
where have you led me,
track within the wood?
To cooling wind, to lifted heart,
to "Yes, I can" and my fresh start,
and everything that's good.

SEEDLINGS
by Abby Oqueli

On the tops of mountains
under the shade of big trees
you reach for the sun.
You push through the earth to
start a fragile life,
weather storms and droughts,
an animal's nibble.

Keep growing – keep reaching
farther into the sky.
Little seedlings, become a
forest.

RAINMAKING
by Lou Piccolo

I sow the seeds
I sow the seeds
I sow the seeds in rows.

I hope the plants
I hope the plants
I hope the plants will grow.

I watch the sky
I watch the sky
I watch the sky for rain.

The day is dry
The day is dry
The day is dry again.

I make it rain
I make it rain
I'm careful not to flood.

Then one day,
I look outside –
yes, I spot a bud!

TEST
by Janet Clare Fagal

My teacher says I'm ready.
My mom says I shouldn't worry.
I've listened hard, practiced.
Done all my work.
And studied.

I remember my teacher's testing tips.
"Be a reading detective,
don't let the questions trick you!
Read them a second time.
Or come back later."

I concentrate
and think things through.
I'm working hard to show what I know.
I focus and stay positive.
I hold onto hope.

THANK-U
by J. David Martinez

A is for Apple
B is for Ball

fast-forward

S is for School
T is for Teacher

rewind

C is for Courage
D is for Diligence

you taught me much more
than reading and writing

much more
than 2 + 2 = 4

you taught me that
hopes + dreams = possibilities

WONDER
by Patricia J. Franz

Hope begins in wonder,
sees possibilities,
kindles curiosity,
sparks a dream of what might be.

It hides in whispered words,
like *I wonder . . . What if? Why?*
Sometimes it sounds like silence,
sometimes a sigh.

You might see hope in hands,
or in somebody's eyes.
Sometimes hope sneaks up on you,
and comes as a surprise.

RESOURCES FOR READERS AND WRITERS

POETRY BOOKS ABOUT HOPE

Poets write about all kinds of topics, but hopefulness is part of nearly all poetry for young people. Some poetry collections, however, focus specifically on the power of hope, dreams, and wishes, such as these books noted here.

Alarcón, Francisco X. 2005. *Poems to Dream Together/Poemas para soñar juntos.*
*Alarcón focuses on family and community through bilingual poems about dreams and goals.

Corcoran, Jill. Ed. 2012. *Dare to Dream . . . Change the World.*
*Each poem highlights a real person who worked toward a big goal and achieved it.

Engle, Margarita. 2012. *The Wild Book.*
*A young girl with dyslexia learns to read and finds freedom through her own personal writing.

Gunning, Monica. 2013. *A Shelter in Our Car.*
*A mother and daughter experiencing homelessness show love and determination.

Heard, Georgia. 2002. Ed. *This Place I Know: Poems of Comfort.*
*Art and poetry by many different creators provide comfort and hope.

Hughes, Langston. (75th anniversary edition) 2007. *The Dream Keeper* (and seven additional poems).
*Classic poems by the great Langston Hughes are full of inspiration.

Nye, Naomi Shihab. Ed. 1992. *This Same Sky: A Collection of Poems from Around the World.*
*Poets from sixty-eight countries offer cross-cultural moments of hope and peace.

Shovan, Laura, 2016. *The Last Fifth Grade of Emerson Elementary.*
*Students rally to save their school from demolition.

Sidman, Joyce. 2009. *Red Sings from Treetops; A Year in Colors.*
*Poems and art focus on the seasons of the year full of sights, sounds, colors, and feelings.

EKPHRASTIC POETRY BOOKS

The books on this list feature poetry written in response to art, called "ekphrastic" poetry.

Brenner, Barbara. Ed. 2000. *Voices: Poetry and Art from Around the World*.
*Poems representing six continents focus on culture, history, or land through art.

Greenberg, Jan. 2001. *Heart to Heart: New Poems Inspired by Twentieth-Century American Art*.
*Paintings, sculpture, and photographs by 20th-century American artists inspire these poems.

Greenberg, Jan. 2008. *Side by Side: New Poems Inspired by Art from Around the World*.
*Poems in their original language and in English accompany global art from ancient Egypt to modern Sweden.

Hopkins, Lee Bennett. Ed. 2018. *World Make Way: New Poems Inspired by Art from the Metropolitan Museum of Art*.
*Poems by eighteen poets inspired by some of the most popular art in the collection of The Metropolitan Museum.

Lewis, J. Patrick and Yolen, Jane. 2011. *Self-Portrait with Seven Fingers: A Life of Marc Chagall in Verse*.
*Fourteen of Chagall's famous paintings are the inspiration for poems by these two poets.

Rochelle, Belinda. Ed. 2001. *Words with Wings: A Treasury of African-American Poetry and Art*.
*Twenty African American poets explore twenty works of art by African American artists on themes of slavery, racism, and pride.

Vardell, Sylvia and Wong, Janet. 2022. *Things We Eat*.
*Poets use photo prompts to explore a wide variety of foods from avocados to kimchi to quiche to zucchini.

Vardell, Sylvia and Wong, Janet. 2022. *What Is a Friend?*
*Poets use photo prompts to explore the many dimensions of friendship.

WEB RESOURCES

Here are some websites that offer engaging activities and helpful resources. Dive in and have fun!

Colorín Colorado
Colorincolorado.org
*Bilingual activities and advice for educators and families of English language learners (ELLs).

Every Child a Reader
everychildareader.net
*Info about book creators, literacy tools and resources, Kids' Book Choice Awards.

Kidlit TV
kidlit.tv
*Videos highlight brand new books and the authors and illustrators who created them.

No Water River
by Renée M. LaTulippe
NoWaterRiver.com
*Watch videos of poets reading and talking about their poetry.

Poetry for Kids
by Kenn Nesbitt
Poetry4Kids.com
*A "poetry playground" with funny poems.

Poetry Foundation
PoetryFoundation.org
*Sponsor of the Young People's Poet Laureate program, with a searchable database that includes some poems for young people.

The Poetry Minute
PoetryMinute.org
*You'll find a poem for every day, Monday through Friday, from September through June.

SHARING POETRY OUT LOUD

It can be fun to read these poems aloud as a group using various informal theater or simple performance techniques.

Simple props can add fun to sharing a poem with a group or larger audience. You can use a common object mentioned in the poem as your "poetry prop" and hold it up while reading aloud. For example, use your cell phone as a prop when reading "Light" (p. 23) or show a stamped, addressed envelope for "Mail" (p. 29) or a fortune cookie for "Fortune" (p. 31) or a gavel for "Benchmark" (p. 41) or any nearby book for "Books" (p. 59).

Consider using audio sound effects or music as a backdrop for a poem reading, where appropriate. For the poem "Drum" (p. 43), play an appropriate musical clip of a drumbeat; for "Ambulance" (p. 63), play the sound of an ambulance's siren; or for "Rainmaking" (p. 81), play the sound of rain falling as you read the poems aloud. One source of sounds and sound effects is SoundCloud.com.

A poem that employs italicized text can be the perfect opportunity for an interactive read-aloud, with a leader or narrator reading most of the poem and others reading the italicized text for added emphasis. One example is "Esperanza" (p. 57) with the key word italicized repeatedly.

Whenever dialogue occurs in a poem, a leader can read most of the poem aloud, with volunteers taking on the parts of dialogue. Take a moment to clarify whose line is whose, highlighting the text if that's helpful. Think about making an audio recording of the reading, too. For example, the columns in "Snap!" (p. 37) can be read by two readers taking turns.

Invite guest readers to join you for the oral reading of a poem to add vocal variety. For example, several of the poems in this book feature animals and scenes from nature, which provides a perfect opportunity to invite a naturalist, park ranger, or outdoors expert to read a poem out loud with us.

POETS WRITE ABOUT WRITING

Several poets have written books ABOUT poetry writing for young people. Here are a few that might be helpful.

Fletcher, Ralph J. 2005. *A Writing Kind of Day: Poems for Young Poets.*
*How to write a poem about almost anything, with tips on every step of the creative process.

Holbrook, Sara, Salinger, Michael and Harvey, Stephanie. 2018. *From Striving to Thriving Writers: Strategies that Jump-Start Writing.*
*Twenty-seven writing strategies and lessons targeting reading, writing, and speaking.

Janeczko, Paul B., comp. 2002. *Seeing the Blue Between: Advice and Inspiration for Young Poets.*
*A poetry collection with poems and advice from 32 poets.

Lawson, JonArno. 2008. *Inside Out: Children's Poets Discuss Their Work.*
*Twenty-three poets sharing poems and explaining how the poem came to be.

Prelutsky, Jack. 2008. *Pizza, Pigs, and Poetry: How to Write a Poem.*
*The poet sharing how he creates poems from anecdotes, often using comic exaggeration.

Salas, Laura Purdie. 2011. *Picture Yourself Writing Poetry: Using Photos to Inspire Writing.*
*A clear and engaging approach with writing prompts and mentor texts.

Wolf, Allan. 2006. *Immersed in Verse: An Informative, Slightly Irreverent & Totally Tremendous Guide to Living the Poet's Life.*
*A poet toolbox full of fun facts, playful writing activities, and words of wisdom and encouragement.

Wong, Janet. 2002. *You Have to Write.*
*A poem picture book emphasizing revision and writing about everyday experiences.

Meet the Author series (published by Richard C. Owen)
Picture books in the "Meet the Author" series feature poets like Douglas Florian, Lee Bennett Hopkins, Janet Wong, and Jane Yolen talking about their lives and how they write poetry.

PLACES TO PUBLISH POETRY

Here are a variety of print and online sources that include poetry by young writers. Be sure to check the rules and specifications for submitting in each venue. Give it a try, have fun, and good luck!

Carus Publishing (Cicada, Cobblestone, Faces, Dig, Muse) (ages 9-14+)
http://www.cobblestonepub.com/index.html
*Magazines on topics from nature to history and more.

New Moon: The Magazine for Girls and Their Dreams (ages 8-14)
http://www.newmoon.com/
*Special online community and magazine for girls.

Skipping Stones (all ages)
http://www.skippingstones.org
*International, multicultural, environmental magazine.

The Claremont Review (ages 13-19)
http://www.theclaremontreview.ca
*International magazine based in Canada.

Stone Soup (ages 8-13)
http://stonesoup.com
*Stories, poems, book reviews, and artwork by young people.

The Telling Room (ages 6-18)
http://www.tellingroom.org/stories
*Publications of annual anthologies, chapbooks, and on the web.

Canvas (ages 8-13)
http://canvasliteraryjournal.com
*Published in print, ebook, web, video, and audio formats.

Writing (grades 7-12)
http://classroommagazines.scholastic.com
*Monthly publication, writing prompts, and writing contests.

PUBLISHED POETRY BY YOUNG WRITERS

Here are several notable collections of poetry written by young people.

Lowe, Ayana. Ed. 2008. *Come and Play: Children of Our World Having Fun.*
*Here are photos of children around the world along with poems by young writers, ages 5-11.

Lyne, Sandford. Ed. 2004. *Soft Hay Will Catch You.*
*Kentucky poet Lyne gathers poems by young writers about home and family.

McLaughlin, Timothy. Ed. 2012. *Walking on Earth and Touching the Sky: Poetry and Prose by Lakota Youth at Red Cloud Indian School.*
*Powerful prose blends with personal poetry by Lakota students at Red Cloud Indian School in South Dakota.

Nye, Naomi Shihab. Ed. 2000. *Salting the Ocean: 100 Poems by Young Poets.*
*Nye collected "100 poems by 100 poets in grades one through twelve."

Simon, John O. Ed. 2011. *Cyclops Wearing Flip-Flops.*
*Students in grades 3-8 respond to classic poems and write their own.

Spain, Sahara Sunday. 2001. *If There Would Be No Light: Poems from My Heart.*
*Dig into these poems by a nine-year-old who has traveled the world.

Stepanek, Mattie. 2002. *Heartsongs.*
*This young poet writes about living with illness and loss.

KINDS OF POEMS

There are several different types of poems in this book, including the following. Just for fun, try writing your own poem in one of these forms.

Free Verse Poem ("Light" p. 23; "Visiting" p. 65; "Military"; p. 75)
Poets who write free verse poems do not use rhyme at the ends of lines, but they often create a rhythm with the length of lines.

List Poem ("Fishing" p. 35; "Test" p. 83)
A list poem incorporates a list of items important to the poem topic.

Mask Poem ("Microscope" p. 25 ; "Help!" p. 69)
A mask poem is written from the point of view of an object, an animal, or a person that is not you (the writer).

Metaphor Poem ("Hurricane" p. 11; "Metamorphosis" p. 17)
The poem compares one thing to another thing that is usually unrelated, but shares attributes.

Poem of Address or Apostrophe Poem ("Ode" p. 73; "Seedlings" p. 79)
The poet "speaks" to the subject of the poem – to an abstract concept or object or a person who is not present.

Poem with Repetition ("Protest" p. 45; "Ambulance" p. 63; "Rainmaking" p. 81)
Poets often repeat a word or phrase or line to emphasize the meaning or to maximize the sounds of the words.

Poem with Rhythm ("Drum" p. 43; "Morning" p. 15)
The poem has a very strong beat of stressed (and unstressed) syllables.

Poem with Simile ("Sculpted" p. 67)
A poem where two or more things are compared with the words "like" or "as" (often a person compared with an animal or object).

Rhyming Poem ("Volunteer" p. 13; "Migration" p. 21)
Many poets use rhyme to emphasize the sounds of words – at the end of lines, in alternating lines, or even in the middle of lines.

Shape Poem ("Plea" p. 71)
The words of the poem are arranged in a shape to suggest the poem's subject.

POETRY AWARDS AND BEST LISTS

There are several major awards given to poets and works of poetry. Knowing about these awards can help you choose what is considered high-quality work.

The **Young People's Poet Laureate (YPPL)** recognizes poets for their body of work. The YPPL consults with the Poetry Foundation and raises awareness of the power of poetry for young people.

Another major award for poetry for children is the **National Council of Teachers of English (NCTE) Award for Excellence in Poetry for Children**, given to a poet for her or his entire body of work in writing or anthologizing poetry for children. Janet Wong is a recent winner of this prestigious award.

Other prominent awards include **The Lee Bennett Hopkins Award for Children's Poetry**, which is presented annually by Pennsylvania State University to an American poet or anthologist for the most outstanding new book of children's poetry published in the previous year.

The Lee Bennett Hopkins/ILA Promising Poet Award goes to a poet with one or two published books, and aims to encourage new poets.

The Claudia Lewis Award is given annually by Bank Street College to the best poetry book of the year.

The Lion and the Unicorn Award for Excellence in North American Poetry is given annually to the best poetry book published in either the U.S. or Canada.

The CYBILS Award (Children's & Young Adult Bloggers' Literary Awards) is given annually to a book of poetry for young people as well as to a novel in verse.

The NCTE Excellence in Poetry Award Committee selects an annual list of **NCTE Poetry Notables** including both poetry books and verse novels.

The CL/R SIG of the International Literacy Association selects an annual list of **Notable Books for a Global Society** for enhancing understanding of world cultures and often includes poetry.

ABOUT THE POETS

You probably found some favorite poems when reading this book. Write down the poets' names and learn more about them by visiting their websites and blogs. Then look for more of their poems (and books)!

Verrena Diane Anderson   newtreemom.wordpress.com
Retired ESL teacher Verrena Diane Anderson writes at her blog, newtreemom. Her "Army brat" son did grow up to become a US Marine.

Dolores Andral   doloresandral.com
Dolores Andral is a mom and an author. She is also a former preschool teacher. She loves sculpting stories for children and adults alike.

Marcie Flinchum Atkins   marcieatkins.com
Marcie Flinchum Atkins is a school librarian and the author of several nonfiction books including *Wait, Rest, Pause: Dormancy in Nature*. She recently saved up enough money to buy a camera to photograph snakes – not take them home as pets.

Rebecca Balcárcel   rebeccabalcarcel.com
Rebecca Balcárcel is the award-winning author of the novels *Shine On, Luz Véliz!,* and *The Other Half of Happy*. She loves popcorn, her kitty, and starting long hikes at dawn.

Robyn Hood Black   robynhoodblack.com
Robyn Hood Black writes and creates in the mountains of South Carolina. She flutters between poetry and art, with each season bringing some new wonder to behold. Learn more about her art at artsyletters.com.

Sandy Brehl   sandybrehlbooks.com
Educator Sandy Brehl writes picture books, poetry, and novels such as the award-winning middle grade WWII trilogy *Odin's Promise*. Having poetry published in Pomelo anthologies is a benchmark in her writing career.

Joseph Bruchac   poetryfoundation.org/poets/joseph-bruchac
Poet and storyteller Joseph Bruchac has published over 180 books in many genres. He's always inspired by the light of possibility in young people's eyes.

Rose Cappelli   imaginethepossibilities.blog
Rose Cappelli is a former reading teacher who writes poems and stories for children. She is always fishing for wonderful words and ideas.

Kelly Conroy   kellyconroy.com
Kelly Conroy writes stories and poems for children. She loves a good space-themed pep talk and hopes the readers will too.

Patricia Cooley   patriciacooley.com
Patricia Cooley is an educator, speaker, author, and storyteller. Her poetry has been published in numerous magazines and anthologies. Patricia uses imagination as her telescope when looking for new and creative ideas.

Cynthia Cotten   cynthiacotten.com
Cynthia Cotten is a poet and author of nine books, including *Snow Ponies* and *This Is the Stable*. She's never found a lost dog but, if she did, she'd do everything she could to get it home again.

Mary E. Cronin   maryecronin.com
Mary E. Cronin is a K-2 Literacy Coach whose poetry has appeared in several anthologies and in *The New York Times*. What makes her hopeful? Books, poems, and good friends.

Linda A. Dryfhout   lindaadryfhout.com
Linda A. Dryfhout's poems appear in numerous magazines and anthologies. The first time she flew, her ears popped! She likes to imagine what it feels like for a child to take their first airplane flight.

Alyssa Eisner   Twitter: @hybridhousewife
When School Library Media Specialist Alyssa Eisner isn't riding her Peloton, tending her garden, feeding her sourdough starter, or trying to keep up with her four kids, she can be found curled up with a good book. She believes poetry is the lighthouse that guides the heart safely home.

Joanne Emery   wordancerblog.com
Poet, photographer, mixed-media artist, and learning specialist, Joanne Emery has encouraged children to use their imaginative powers for over forty years. She has hope in this new generation to live peacefully and creatively.

Lauren Emick
Dr. Lauren Emick is a teacher, scholar, and poet. She finds inspiration for hope in her own students as they navigate exciting challenges, such as tug-of-war on Field Day.

Janet Clare Fagal   Facebook: facebook.com/janet.clare.311
Janet Clare Fagal's poems appear in several anthologies and at nlapw.org. For many years she taught third and fifth graders to love poetry, and worked to build their confidence and test-taking savvy by showing them how to be "reading detectives" on test days.

Patricia J. Franz   patriciajfranz.com
Patricia J. Franz finds hope in poetry, picture books, wildflowers, and boxes! Her poetry appears in *What Is a Friend?*, *Things We Wear*, and *Things We Feel*.

Theresa Gaughan   Twitter: @TheresaGaughan
Theresa Gaughan is a veteran teacher who enjoys sharing poetry with her third-grade students. She is grateful for ambulance workers who come to the aid of people who are injured or ill.

Stephanie Gimble
Stephanie Gimble has been a Children's Librarian for thirty years. She loves children, she loves poetry, and she loves children's poetry. Her favorite protest song is "Blowin' in the Wind."

Sherilyn Howard   Instagram: @jinxyrad
Librarian Sherilyn Howard reads and writes poetry for enjoyment and encourages her students to do the same. The first day of school every year made her so nervous, her stomach churned like a hurricane.

Elizabeth Kuelbs   elizabethkuelbs.com
Elizabeth Kuelbs writes stories and poems for children and adults. She thinks it's fun to imagine what it would be like to shrink to microscopic size and go swimming with tardigrades.

Jone Rush MacCulloch   jonerushmacculloch.com
A poet, photographer, artist, former library media teacher, Jone Rush MacCulloch blogs for Poetry Friday. Her day begins by taking photos of the sunrise and doing Wordle. Having nurses in her family, she has a deep appreciation for hospitals.

Vikram Madan   vikrammadan.com
Vikram Madan is the author-illustrator of the acclaimed poetry collection *A Hatful of Dragons: And More Than 13.8 Billion Other Funny Poems*. Every morning he looks forward to reading new poems by other poets.

J. David Martinez
J. David Martinez is an ELA teacher in Fort Worth, Texas. He'd like to say "Thank-U" to the teachers along the way who helped him open the door to possibilities!

Rochelle Melander   rochellemelander.com
Writing coach and artist educator Rochelle Melander is the author of 12 books, including *Mightier Than the Sword* – an ode to people who've changed the world through writing.

Kenn Nesbitt   poetry4kids.com
Former Children's Poet Laureate (2013-15) Kenn Nesbitt is the author of more than 25 books for kids, mostly funny poems. He loves the suspense of not knowing what he will write next.

Abby Oqueli   mrsoqueli@edublogs.org
Middle school English teacher of 14 years and classroom poet Abby Oqueli is a globetrotting educator. She splits her time between the seedlings in her classroom and the ones she made from scratch.

Lou Piccolo   loupiccolo.com
Lou Piccolo is an editor and author of children's literature. She writes graded readers for the educational market and contributes to children's magazines. Lou believes in making, making, making her own luck.

Deborah Reidy   linkedin.com/in/deborah-reidy-1ab979b9/
In the classroom Deborah Reidy loved helping students write poetry. Today she has the good fortune to be a poet herself, with many of her poems published in children's magazines and anthologies.

Suma Subramaniam   sumasubramaniam.com
Suma Subramaniam's books include *Namaste Is a Greeting*, *She Sang for India*, and *The Runaway Dosa*. Every night, her wild imagination spins and swirls stories for children.

Linda Picaro Tarantino
As an Early Childhood Education Specialist from PreK to college, Linda Picaro Tarantino has devoted herself to motivating creativity in children. She enjoys writing, painting, fiber arts, and traveling. Humorous, fun, and playful poems are her specialty!

Pamela Taylor   pamelabtaylor.com
Former educator Pamela Taylor has poems featured in *Things We Feel, What Is a Family?,* and *What Is a Friend?* (anthologies published by Pomelo Books). Her favorite cat was Mousetrap and he didn't have any fleas.

Linda Kulp Trout   lindakulptrout.blogspot.com
Linda Kulp Trout s a teacher and poet. Her poems appear in many anthologies and a forthcoming novel in verse. She loves receiving handwritten letters in the mail.

Joyce Uglow   inkingcompellingstories.com
Joyce Uglow, poet and picture book author, digs in on topics from bees, trees, and families to ancient asphalt seeps that reveal stories. She plants hope for our planet.

Vicki Wilke   winningwriters.com/people/vicki-wilke
Vicki Wilke taught K-1 for 33 years. She has been published in many anthologies for children and adults. Her five grandchildren are precious to her, and she loves their migration to Michigan for happy reunions!

Matthew Winter   Twitter: @Baileysdad420
Matthew Winter is an elementary school teacher who loves to get lost in a good book (poetry included) while his poodle-son Bailey is curled by his side. He has poems published in *What Is a Friend?* and *What Is a Family?*

Sarah Ziman   sarahziman.co.uk
Sarah Ziman is an award-winning poet from the UK whose work appears regularly in magazines and anthologies. She loves to do volunteer work such as litter picking, especially together with friends.

POEM CREDITS

Verrena Diane Anderson: "Military"; © 2023 by Verrena Diane Anderson.
Dolores Andral: "Sculpted"; © 2023 by Dolores Andral.
Marcie Flinchum Atkins: "Money"; © 2023 by Marcie Flinchum Atkins.
Rebecca Balcárcel: "Hike"; © 2023 by Rebecca Balcárcel.
Robyn Hood Black: "Metamorphosis"; © 2023 by Robyn Hood Black.
Sandy Brehl: "Benchmark"; © 2023 by Sandy Brehl.
Joseph Bruchac: "Light"; © 2023 by Joseph Bruchac
Rose Cappelli: "Fishing"; © 2023 by Rose Cappelli.
Kelly Conroy: "Rocket"; © 2023 by Kelly Conroy.
Patricia Cooley: "Telescope"; © 2023 by Patricia Cooley.
Cynthia Cotten: "Lost"; © 2023 by Cynthia Cotten.
Mary E. Cronin: "Drum"; © 2023 by Mary E. Cronin.
Linda A. Dryfhout: "Airport"; © 2023 by Linda A. Dryfhout.
Alyssa Eisner: "Lighthouse"; © 2023 by Alyssa Eisner.
Joanne Emery: "Esperanza"; © 2023 by Joanne Emery.
Lauren Emick: "Tug-of-War"; © 2023 by Lauren Emick.
Janet Clare Fagal: "Test"; © 2023 by Janet Clare Fagal.
Patricia J. Franz: "Wonder"; © 2023 by Patricia J. Franz.
Theresa Gaughan: "Ambulance"; © 2023 by Theresa Gaughan.
Stephanie Gimble: "Protest"; © 2023 by Stephanie Gimble.
Sherilyn Howard: "Hurricane"; © 2023 by Sherilyn Howard.
Elizabeth Kuelbs: "Microscope"; © 2023 by Elizabeth Kuelbs.
Jone Rush MacCulloch: "Visiting"; © 2023 by Jone Rush MacCulloch.
Vikram Madan: "Morning"; © 2023 by Vikram Madan.
J. David Martinez: "Thank-U"; © 2023 by J. David Martinez.
Rochelle Melander: "Ode"; © 2023 by Rochelle Melander.
Kenn Nesbitt: "Suspense"; © 2023 by Kenn Nesbitt.
Abby Oqueli: "Seedlings"; © 2023 by Abby Oqueli.
Lou Piccolo: "Rainmaking"; © 2023 by Louanne Piccolo.
Deborah Reidy: "Fortune"; © 2023 by Deborah S. Reidy.
Suma Subramaniam: "Flight"; © 2023 by Suma Subramaniam.
Linda Picaro Tarantino: "Wheels"; © 2023 by Linda Picaro Tarantino.
Pamela Taylor: "Plea"; © 2023 by Pamela Taylor.
Linda Kulp Trout: "Mail"; © 2023 by Linda Kulp Trout.
Joyce Uglow: "Snap!"; © 2023 by Joyce Uglow.
Sylvia Vardell: "World"; © 2023 by Sylvia M. Vardell.
Vicki Wilke: "Migration"; © 2023 by Vicki Wilke.
Matthew Winter: "Books"; © 2023 by Matthew Winter.
Janet Wong: "Pickleball"; © 2023 by Janet S. Wong.
Sarah Ziman: "Volunteer"; © 2023 by Sarah Ziman.

These poems are used with the permission of the author, with all rights reserved. To request reprint rights, please send an email to info@pomelobooks.com and we'll connect you with the poets.

ABOUT VARDELL & WONG

Sylvia M. Vardell recently retired as Professor in the School of Library and Information Studies at Texas Woman's University where she taught graduate courses in children's and young adult literature for more than 20 years. Vardell has published extensively, including five books on literature for children as well as over 25 book chapters and 100 journal articles. Her poem reflects her worry about the world, as well as the hope she finds in friends, puppies, and homemade cookies! Learn more about Vardell at SylviaVardell.com.

Janet Wong is a graduate of Yale Law School and a former lawyer. She has written more than 40 books for children on a wide variety of subjects, including chess (*Alex and the Wednesday Chess Club*) and yoga (*Twist: Yoga Poems*). She is the 2021 winner of the NCTE Excellence in Poetry for Children Award, a lifetime achievement award that is one of the highest honors a children's poet can receive. One of Janet's favorite activities is pickleball; she feels filled with hope at the start of each game. Learn more about Janet at Janet-Wong.com.

Together, Vardell & Wong are the creative forces behind Pomelo Books, a publisher whose "family" of authors includes more than 250 poets.

ABOUT POMELO BOOKS

Pomelo Books is Poetry PLUS. Poetry PLUS play. Poetry PLUS science. Poetry PLUS holidays. Poetry PLUS pets – and more. We make it EASY to share poetry any time of day.

Successful K-12 teachers and administrators build regular "touch points" into their routines to create a safe and engaging learning environment. Poetry can be a powerful tool for offering a shared literary experience in just a few minutes, with both curricular benefits and emotional connections for students at all levels.

Our books in *The Poetry Friday Anthology* series and the *Poetry Friday Power Book* series make it easy to use poetry for integrating skills, building language learning, crossing curricular areas, mentoring young writers, promoting critical thinking, fostering social-emotional development, and inviting students to respond creatively. A shared poetry moment can help build a classroom community filled with kindness, respect, and joy. Learn more at PomeloBooks.com.

The Poetry of Science
An NSTA Recommends selection
"A treasury of the greatest science poetry for children ever written, with a twist." NSTA

The Poetry of Science is an illustrated book for children that contains 250 poems on science, technology, engineering, and math organized by topic.

GREAT MORNING! Poems for School Leaders to Read Aloud
A CBC Hot Off the Press selection

75 poems for morning announcements or for the start of class or just to take a "brain break" when you need it! Principals, teachers, and student leaders will find poems on many useful topics from school safety to celebrating the teamwork of teachers and staff members such as the school nurse or custodian.

HERE WE GO: A Poetry Friday Power Book
An NCTE Poetry Notable
An NNSTOY Social Justice Book

How can kids change the world? By practicing kindness, raising a garden that unites a community, thinking about the news, and more. This story in poems (with activities to get us drawing, talking, and writing) will guide kids as they discover their power to make an impact.

MORE FROM POMELO BOOKS

HOP TO IT: Poems to Get You Moving
A Kids' Book Choice Award "Best Book of Facts" Winner

This anthology of 100 poems by 90 poets gets kids thinking and moving as they use pantomime, sign language, and whole body movements, including deskercise! You'll also find poems on "21st-century" topics, such as life during a pandemic. Take a 30-second indoor recess whenever you need it!

The Poetry Friday Anthology for Celebrations
ILA Notable Books for a Global Society

This fun book features 156 poems (in both Spanish & English) honoring a wide variety of traditional and non-traditional holidays from all over the world. Also available in a Teacher/Librarian Edition.

"A bubbly and educational bilingual poetry anthology for children." – Kirkus

What Is a Friend?
A CBC Hot Off the Press selection

Forty-one poems by recognized poets and new talents explore the many aspects of friendship, including friendship with pets, teammates as friends, friends who are family members, and much more.

What Is a Family?

Forty poems by recognized poets and new talents explore the many aspects of family, including blended families, relationships with parents, siblings, aunts, uncles, and grandparents, and families found within neighborhoods, classrooms, marching bands, sports teams, and clubs.

www.ingramcontent.com/pod-product-compliance
Lightning Source LLC
Chambersburg PA
CBHW041130110526
44592CB00020B/2754